CENTRAL BANKS

A History

Dan Wilson

ISBN-13: 9798388218025

Cover design by: Dan Wilson

PREFACE

"Central Banks: A History" provides a comprehensive overview of central banks, their history, governance, and goals. It offers insights into the similarities and differences between various central banks around the world, highlighting the unique challenges and opportunities facing each institution.

By exploring the origins and evolution of central banking, as well as contemporary issues and criticisms, this book provides a valuable resource for anyone seeking to understand the role of central banks in the global economy. Whether you are a student, a financial professional, or simply curious about the workings of the global financial

Central banks have been an integral part of the global economy for centuries, playing a key role in shaping economic growth, stability, and prosperity. From the Federal Reserve Bank of the United States to the Bank of Japan and the European Central Bank, each central bank has its own unique history, governance structure, and approach to achieving its goals.

This book explores the origins, evolution, and contemporary issues of several key central banks around the world, including the goals, structures, transparency, and accountability of each bank. It also delves into some of the criticisms and challenges facing central banks today, as well as some interesting facts about their unique characteristics.

As the global economy continues to evolve, the role of central banks remains as important as ever. This book aims to provide an accessible and informative introduction to the world of central banking, offering insights into the complexities, challenges, and opportunities facing these institutions.

Whether you are a student of economics, a financial professional, or simply curious about the role of central banks in the global economy, this book will provide valuable insights into this fascinating and important topic.

INTRODUCTION

Central banks play a crucial role in the global economy, influencing the supply of money and credit, setting interest rates, and managing the stability of financial systems. From the Federal Reserve Bank in the United States to the European Central Bank, and from the Bank of Japan to the Reserve Bank of India, central banks have a long and complex history.

In this book, we have explored the origins and evolution of some of the world's most significant central banks, discussing their goals, structures, transparency, accountability, and ownership. We also examined some of the criticisms and challenges facing central banks today, as well as some interesting facts that shed light on their unique characteristics.

The idea of central banks dates back to the 17th century, when various European countries established institutions to manage their national currencies and provide financial stability. The Swedish Riksbank, founded in 1668, is often considered the world's first central bank. Other early central banks include the Bank of England, founded in 1694, and the Bank of France, founded in 1800. The United States established its first central bank, the First Bank of the United States, in 1791.

The first central banks were established in Europe in the late 17th and early 18th centuries, with the primary goal of providing financial stability and promoting economic growth. Here are some of the early European central banks and their histories:

1. Riksbank (Sweden, 1668): The Riksbank is often considered the world's first central bank. It was established by the Swedish parliament to stabilize the country's currency and promote trade. Its original functions included issuing banknotes, managing the currency supply, and lending to the government.

2. Bank of England (England, 1694): The Bank of England was founded to raise funds for the government to fight a war against France. It was initially a private bank, but it became the central bank of England in the 18th century. Its primary functions were to manage the government's debt, issue banknotes, and regulate commercial banks.

3. Bank of France (France, 1800): The Bank of France was established to stabilize the country's finances after the French Revolution. Its primary functions were to issue banknotes, manage the currency supply, and regulate the banking system.

4. Reichsbank (Germany, 1876): The Reichsbank was established by the German Empire to manage the country's currency and promote economic growth. Its primary functions were to issue banknotes, manage the currency supply, and lend to the government.

5. Banca d'Italia (Italy, 1893): The Banca d'Italia was established to stabilize Italy's currency and promote economic growth. Its primary functions were to issue banknotes, manage the currency supply, and regulate the banking system.

These early European central banks played a crucial role in shaping modern banking and finance. They helped to establish a stable monetary system, promote economic growth, and manage government debt. Over time, central banks have taken on additional responsibilities, such as regulating banks, conducting monetary policy, and managing financial crises.

After the establishment of the first central banks in Europe, other countries around the world followed suit and established their own central banks. Here are some of the key central banks that were established after the ones mentioned earlier:

1. Federal Reserve (United States, 1913): The Federal Reserve was established to stabilize the US financial system and prevent banking crises. Its primary functions include conducting monetary policy, regulating banks, and managing the currency supply.

2. Bank of Japan (Japan, 1882): The Bank of Japan was established to manage the country's currency and promote economic growth. Its primary functions include conducting monetary policy, managing the currency supply, and regulating banks.

3. Reserve Bank of India (India, 1935): The Reserve Bank of India was established to manage the country's currency and promote economic growth. Its primary functions include conducting monetary policy, managing the currency supply, and regulating banks.

4. People's Bank of China (China, 1948): The People's Bank of China was established to manage the country's currency and promote economic growth. Its primary functions include conducting monetary policy, managing the currency supply, and regulating banks.

5. European Central Bank (Eurozone, 1998): The European Central Bank was established to manage monetary policy for the Eurozone countries that use the euro as their currency. Its primary functions

include conducting monetary policy, managing the currency supply, and promoting financial stability.

These central banks, along with others that have been established around the world, play a critical role in managing monetary policy, regulating financial institutions, and promoting economic growth.

EARLY CENTRAL BANKS

Riksbank

the Riksbank is still in operation today and remains the central bank of Sweden. It was founded by the Swedish parliament in 1668, making it the oldest central bank in the world. The bank's name, "Riksbank", means "national bank" in Swedish.

The Riksbank was originally established to stabilize Sweden's currency and promote trade. Over the years, its role has expanded to include managing monetary policy, regulating the financial system, and promoting financial stability. Today, the Riksbank is responsible for setting interest rates, managing the country's currency reserves, and overseeing payment systems.

The Riksbank is governed by a board of directors, which is responsible for setting monetary policy and managing the bank's operations. The board consists of six members, including the governor of the Riksbank, who is appointed by the Swedish government.

Bank of England

SEALING OF THE BANK OF ENGLAND CHARTER. 1694.

SIR JOHN HOUBLON,
Governor.

SIR JOHN SOMERS,
Lord Keeper.

MR. MICHAEL GODFREY
Deputy Governor.

Public Domain Image 1

The Bank of England is still in operation today and remains the central bank of the United Kingdom. It was founded in 1694, making it the second oldest central bank in the world after the Riksbank in Sweden.

The Bank of England's primary functions include managing monetary policy, regulating the financial system, and promoting financial stability. It is responsible for setting interest rates, managing the country's currency reserves, and overseeing payment systems. The Bank also serves as the banker and debt manager for the UK government.

The Bank of England is governed by a board of directors, which is responsible for setting monetary policy and managing the bank's operations. The board consists of the governor of the Bank of England, who is appointed by the British government, and two deputy governors, as well as other members who are appointed by the governor and approved by the government.

The key people who started the Bank of England were a group of wealthy businessmen led by William Paterson, a Scottish merchant and financier. In 1691, Paterson proposed the idea of establishing a national bank to the English government, arguing that such a bank would help to finance the country's debt and provide a stable source of credit for businesses.

The English government initially rejected Paterson's proposal, but they eventually agreed to establish the bank in 1694 as a way to finance the country's war against France. The bank was initially owned by a group of private investors, with the government purchasing a 50% stake in the bank in 1946 and nationalizing it fully in 1946.

The Bank of England's first governor was Sir John Houblon, a prominent London merchant and banker. Other key figures in the bank's early history included Michael Godfrey, the first deputy governor, and Thomas Neale, a wealthy entrepreneur who helped to finance the bank's early operations.

Bank of France

The Bank of France, or Banque de France in French, is the central bank of France. It was founded in 1800, shortly after the French Revolution, with the aim of stabilizing the country's financial system and promoting economic growth.

The Bank of France's primary functions include managing monetary policy, regulating the banking system, and promoting financial stability. It is responsible for setting interest rates, managing the country's currency reserves, and overseeing payment systems.

The Bank of France is governed by a board of directors, which is responsible for setting monetary policy and managing the bank's operations. The board consists of the governor of the Bank of France, who is appointed by the French government, and four deputy governors, as well as other members who are appointed by the governor and approved by the government.

Over the years, the Bank of France has played a significant role in shaping the French economy and financial system. It has helped to finance government debt, promote economic growth, and provide stability during financial crises. Today, the Bank of France is an important player in the global financial system and works closely with other central banks and international organizations to promote financial stability and economic growth.

The Rothschild family was involved in the establishment of several central banks around the world, but they did not directly create any of them.

In the late 18th and early 19th centuries, the Rothschilds became one of the most prominent banking families in Europe, and they played a significant role in financing governments and other institutions. Their connections and financial resources made them key players in the establishment of several central banks, including the Bank of England, the Bank of France, and the Reichsbank in Germany.

For example, Nathan Mayer Rothschild, the head of the London branch of the family's banking business, was instrumental in helping to finance the British government's war against Napoleon. He also helped to secure the Bank of England's monopoly on the issuance of banknotes in the early 19th century.

Similarly, James Mayer de Rothschild, the head of the Paris branch of the family's business, played a key role in the establishment of the Bank of France in 1800. The Rothschilds' connections and financial expertise helped to establish these central banks and cement their role in the global financial system.

Reichsbank

The Reichsbank is no longer in operation as it was dissolved in 1945 following the defeat of Nazi Germany in World War II. It was replaced by the Deutsche Bundesbank, which became the central bank of West Germany.

The Reichsbank was created in 1876 by the German Empire, with the aim of managing the country's currency and promoting economic growth. Its primary functions included issuing banknotes, managing the currency supply, and lending to the government.

Over the years, the Reichsbank played a significant role in shaping the German economy and financial system. It helped to finance government debt, promote economic growth, and provide stability during financial crises. However, during World War II, the Reichsbank was closely tied to the Nazi regime and played a role in financing its war effort.

Following the war, the Allied powers dissolved the Reichsbank and replaced it with new central banks in both East and West Germany. The Deutsche Bundesbank, established in 1957, became the central bank of West Germany and later of the unified Germany after the fall of the Berlin Wall in 1989.

The Deutsche Bundesbank is the central bank of Germany and

operates independently under the control of its own executive board. The executive board is responsible for the day-to-day operations of the bank and consists of six members, including the president of the bank.

The Deutsche Bundesbank's primary functions include managing monetary policy, regulating the banking system, and promoting financial stability. It is responsible for setting interest rates, managing the country's currency reserves, and overseeing payment systems.

The Deutsche Bundesbank is governed by a supervisory board, which consists of the bank's president, the executive board members, and representatives from the German government and the country's regional central banks. The supervisory board is responsible for setting the bank's strategic direction and overseeing its activities.

As the central bank of Germany, the Deutsche Bundesbank plays a critical role in shaping the country's economy and financial system. It works closely with other central banks and international organizations to promote financial stability and economic growth, and its policies have a significant impact on the broader European economy as well.

Banca d'Italia

The Banca d'Italia, or Bank of Italy in English, was established in 1893 by the Italian government with the aim of stabilizing the country's currency and promoting economic growth.

At the time, Italy had only recently become a unified country, and its banking system was fragmented and unstable. The government recognized the need for a central bank to provide a stable source of credit for businesses, regulate the banking system, and manage the country's currency.

The Banca d'Italia was created by merging several existing banks, including the Banca Nazionale nel Regno d'Italia and the Banca Toscana, into a single institution. The new bank was given the exclusive right to issue banknotes in Italy and was responsible for managing the country's currency supply.

Over the years, the Banca d'Italia played a significant role in shaping the Italian economy and financial system. It helped to finance government debt, promote economic growth, and provide stability during financial crises. Today, the Banca d'Italia is an important player in the global financial system and works closely with other central banks and international organizations to promote financial stability and economic growth.

THE FEDERAL RESERVE

The creation of the Federal Reserve was the result of a long process that involved many key figures in the US government, banking industry, and academia. Here are some of the most notable individuals who played a role in the creation of the Federal Reserve:

1. Nelson Aldrich: As a Republican senator from Rhode Island, Aldrich was instrumental in drafting the Federal Reserve Act of 1913, which created the Federal Reserve system. He was also the chairman of the National Monetary Commission, which conducted extensive research on the US banking system and recommended the creation of a central bank.

2. Woodrow Wilson: As the President of the United States, Wilson signed the Federal Reserve Act into law in 1913. He supported the creation of a central bank and saw it as a way to provide greater stability to the US financial system.

3. Paul Warburg: A German-born banker and financier, Warburg was a leading advocate for the creation of a central bank in the United States. He was a member of the National Monetary Commission and played a key role in drafting the Federal Reserve Act. Warburg later became one of the first governors of the Federal Reserve Board.

4. Carter Glass: As a Democratic congressman from Virginia, Glass co-sponsored the Federal Reserve Act

and played a key role in its passage through Congress. He later became the first Secretary of the Treasury under the Federal Reserve system.

5. Benjamin Strong: Strong was the first governor of the Federal Reserve Bank of New York, which became the most powerful of the 12 regional Federal Reserve banks. He played a key role in shaping the Fed's policies and was instrumental in stabilizing the US financial system during the 1920s.

These individuals, along with many others, played a crucial role in the creation of the Federal Reserve system and helped to shape the US financial system as we know it today.

Several of the key figures involved in the creation of the Federal Reserve system met at the **Jekyll Island** resort in Georgia in November 1910. The group, which included Senator Nelson Aldrich, Paul Warburg, and other prominent bankers and financiers, met in secret to discuss the need for a central banking system in the United States.

The Jekyll Island meeting was significant because it provided a forum for these individuals to discuss their ideas and work out the details of what would become the Federal Reserve Act of 1913. The group's discussions and proposals formed the basis for the National Monetary Commission's report on banking reform, which in turn led to the creation of the Federal Reserve system.

While the Jekyll Island meeting has been the subject of much speculation and controversy over the years, there is no doubt that it played an important role in the development of the Federal Reserve system. Many of the individuals who attended the meeting went on to play key roles in the drafting and passage of the Federal Reserve Act, and their ideas helped to shape the structure and function of the Fed as we know it today.

The **Sixteenth Amendment** to the US Constitution, which authorized the federal income tax, was actually passed in 1913, the same year as the Federal Reserve Act. The income tax was seen as an important source of revenue for the federal government and helped to provide a stable source of funding for the Federal Reserve system.

While the income tax was not directly related to the creation of the Federal Reserve, it did play an important role in shaping the financial system of the United States. The income tax provided the federal government with a stable source of revenue, which in turn allowed it to issue bonds and other securities that could be purchased by the Federal Reserve.

The Federal Reserve buys Treasury securities as a way of managing the money supply and controlling interest rates. When the Fed buys Treasuries, it injects money into the economy, which can help to stimulate economic growth. The Treasuries are paid back to the Fed with interest, which provides a source of revenue for the central bank.

So while the income tax was not directly tied to the creation of the Federal Reserve, it did play an important role in shaping the financial system of the United States and providing a stable source of funding for the government and the central bank.

There are twelve regional Federal Reserve Banks in the Federal Reserve system, located in different parts of the United States. These regional banks are responsible for implementing the policies set by the Federal Reserve Board, which is the central governing body of the Federal Reserve system.

The twelve Federal Reserve Banks are located in Boston, New York, Philadelphia, Cleveland, Richmond, Atlanta, Chicago, St. Louis, Minneapolis, Kansas City, Dallas, and San Francisco. Each bank is responsible for carrying out the Federal Reserve's policies and functions within its designated region.

In addition to the regional banks, the Federal Reserve also includes the Federal Reserve Board, which is located in Washington, D.C., and is responsible for setting monetary policy and overseeing the operations of the regional banks. The Federal Open Market Committee (FOMC), which includes members of the Federal Reserve Board and presidents of some of the regional banks, is responsible for setting interest rates and implementing other monetary policies.

The **Federal Open Market Committee (FOMC)** is the main policymaking body of the Federal Reserve System. It is responsible for making decisions on monetary policy, including setting the target for the federal funds rate, which is the interest rate that banks charge each other for overnight loans.

The FOMC is composed of twelve members, including the seven members of the Federal Reserve Board and five of the twelve regional Federal Reserve Bank presidents. The president of the Federal Reserve Bank of New York is a permanent member of the FOMC, while the other four regional bank presidents rotate on a yearly basis.

The Federal Reserve Board members, including the Chair of the Federal Reserve, have permanent voting rights on the FOMC, while the regional bank presidents serve rotating terms as voting members. The Chair of the FOMC is selected from among the members of the Federal Reserve Board and serves a four-year term.

The FOMC meets eight times a year to assess economic conditions and make decisions on monetary policy. During these meetings, the committee reviews data on employment, inflation, and other key economic indicators to determine whether to adjust interest rates or take other policy actions.

The regional bank presidents play an important role in these meetings by providing insights into local economic conditions and advocating for policy decisions that reflect the needs of their respective regions. The Federal Reserve Board members, on the other hand, bring expertise in finance and economics to the table and are responsible for setting the overall direction of monetary policy.

The FOMC plays a critical role in shaping US monetary policy and is closely watched by financial markets and policymakers around the world. Its decisions can have a significant impact on the US economy and global financial markets.

The president of the Federal Reserve Bank of New York is a **permanent voting member**, while the other four regional bank presidents rotate on a yearly basis as voting members.

The Federal Reserve Bank of New York is the largest and most influential of the 12 regional Federal Reserve Banks, and it plays a unique role in the US financial system. Because of its importance, the president of the New York Fed is a permanent voting member of the Federal Open Market Committee (FOMC).

The New York Fed is responsible for implementing the Federal Reserve's monetary policy decisions in the financial markets. It also acts as the Fed's eyes and ears on Wall Street, monitoring financial conditions and providing insights into the workings of the US financial system. The New York Fed is also responsible for executing the Fed's open market operations, which involve buying and selling government securities to influence the money supply and interest rates.

Given the New York Fed's important role in the US financial system and its close proximity to Wall Street, having the president of the New York Fed as a permanent voting member of the FOMC ensures that the committee has access to up-to-date information and insights into financial market conditions. This helps the FOMC to make informed decisions about monetary policy and respond quickly to changing economic conditions.

In addition to the president of the New York Fed, four other regional Federal Reserve Bank presidents serve as voting members of the FOMC on a rotating basis, with each president serving a one-year term.

All FOMC members attend the meetings, which are held eight times per year in Washington D.C. However, only the voting members of the committee are allowed to cast votes on monetary policy decisions. The voting members typically include the seven members of the Federal Reserve Board and the rotating group of four regional bank presidents.

In addition to the voting members, the FOMC meetings are also attended by a number of non-voting participants, including the presidents of the other regional Federal Reserve Banks, as well as economists, staff members, and other experts who provide input and analysis to the committee. The meetings are also open to observers and members of the public, although attendance is limited and must be arranged in advance.

The FOMC meetings are closely watched by financial markets

and policymakers around the world, as the committee's decisions can have a significant impact on the US economy and global financial markets. The meetings provide an important forum for policymakers to assess economic conditions, make decisions on monetary policy, and communicate their decisions to the public.

Shares in the Federal Reserve are not publicly traded and cannot be bought or sold on the open market. Instead, the Federal Reserve is owned by the member banks of the Federal Reserve System, which are privately owned commercial banks located throughout the United States.

When a bank becomes a member of the Federal Reserve System, it is required to purchase stock in its regional Federal Reserve Bank. This stock is not traded on any exchange and has no market value. Instead, it serves as a membership requirement and gives the member banks certain rights and privileges, including the ability to vote for the directors of their regional Federal Reserve Bank and receive dividends on their stock.

The amount of stock that a member bank must purchase is determined by the size of the bank and the amount of deposits it holds. The stock is not transferable and cannot be sold or traded, and it is not a claim on the assets of the Federal Reserve or its member banks. Instead, it represents a small ownership interest in the regional Federal Reserve Bank and gives the member bank a voice in the governance of the Federal Reserve System.

Some of the profits generated by the Federal Reserve's holdings of Treasury securities are paid to its member banks in the form of dividends on their stock holdings in the regional Federal Reserve Banks.

The Federal Reserve System has over 5,000 member banks, including some of the largest banks in the United States. Some of the largest member banks of the Federal Reserve include:

1. JPMorgan Chase: JPMorgan Chase is the largest bank in the United States by assets and is a member of the Federal Reserve System.

2. Bank of America: Bank of America is the second-largest bank in the United States by assets and is also a member of the Federal Reserve System.

3. Wells Fargo: Wells Fargo is the fourth-largest bank in the United States by assets and is a member of the Federal Reserve System.

4. Citibank: Citibank is the fifth-largest bank in the United States by assets and is also a member of the Federal Reserve System.

5. U.S. Bancorp: U.S. Bancorp is the sixth-largest bank in the United States by assets and is a member of the Federal Reserve System.

There is no specific limit to how much member banks of the Federal Reserve can be paid from profits generated by the Fed's holdings of US Treasury notes, bonds, and bills. However, the amount of dividends paid to member banks is determined by the Federal Reserve Act, which sets a fixed rate of 6% per year on the stock held by member banks in their regional Federal Reserve Banks.

Under the Federal Reserve Act, the Federal Reserve's net earnings are first used to pay its operating expenses. Any remaining profits are then remitted to the US Treasury. Before these profits are remitted to the Treasury, a portion of them is used to pay dividends to the member banks based on their holdings of stock in their regional Federal Reserve Bank.

While there is no specific limit on the amount of dividends that can be paid to member banks, the Federal Reserve is required to operate in a financially responsible manner and maintain adequate capital to carry out its functions. The Fed is subject to regular audits and oversight by Congress to ensure that it is operating in a safe and sound manner and in the best interests of the US economy.

These banks, along with many others, hold stock in their regional Federal Reserve Banks and play an important role in the governance of the Federal Reserve System. As members of the Fed, they have access to a wide range of financial services, including access to the Fed's discount window and the ability to participate in open market operations.

Each year, after covering its operating expenses, the Federal Reserve returns the remaining profits from its operations to the US Treasury. However, before these profits are remitted to the Treasury, a portion of them is used to pay dividends to the member banks.

The Federal Reserve Act specifies that member banks are entitled to receive a dividend on their stock holdings in the Federal Reserve Banks equal to 6% per year. This dividend is paid out of the profits generated by the Federal Reserve's operations, including the interest earned on Treasury securities held in the Fed's portfolio.

These dividends do not represent a direct transfer of funds from the US Treasury to the member banks (Like BofA, Chase, Wells Fargo). Instead, they are paid out of the Federal Reserve's earnings and represent a return on the member banks' investment in the regional Federal Reserve Banks. The amount of the dividend payment is determined by the amount of stock held by each member bank in their regional Federal Reserve Bank.

The profits of the Federal Reserve are made public. Each year, the Federal Reserve publishes an audited financial statement, which provides detailed information on the Fed's balance sheet, income statement, and cash flows for the previous year.

The annual financial statement includes information on the Fed's assets and liabilities, including its holdings of US Treasury securities and other securities, as well as its lending activities, reserve balances, and other financial data. The statement also includes information on the amount of profits generated by the Federal Reserve during the year and the amount of dividends paid to member banks.

In addition to the annual financial statement, the Federal Reserve publishes regular reports and updates on its activities and operations, including reports on monetary policy, financial stability, and economic developments. These reports are widely disseminated and provide important insights into the Fed's thinking and decision-making processes.

It is not accurate to describe the Federal Reserve as a private bank. While the Federal Reserve System includes 12 regional Federal Reserve Banks, which are private institutions owned by their member banks, the Federal Reserve as a whole is a quasi-public institution that operates as an independent agency within the federal government.

The Federal Reserve is subject to oversight by Congress. The Federal Reserve Board, which is the central governing body of the Federal Reserve System, consists of seven members who are appointed by the President of the United States and confirmed by the Senate. The Chair of the Federal Reserve Board is also appointed by the President and confirmed by the Senate.

While the member banks of the Federal Reserve System do hold stock in their regional Federal Reserve Banks, this does not give them control over the Federal Reserve's policy decisions or operations. The Federal Reserve's monetary policy decisions are made independently by the Federal Open Market Committee (FOMC), which is composed of members of the Federal Reserve Board and regional Federal Reserve Bank presidents. The FOMC operates independently of political influence and makes its decisions based on its assessment of economic conditions and its mandate to promote price stability and full employment.

When the Federal Reserve System was created in 1913, the members of the Federal Reserve Board were referred to as "governors," while the presidents of the regional Federal Reserve Banks were referred to as "directors." This terminology reflected the fact that the Federal Reserve was modeled in part on the structure of central banks in Europe, where the heads of central banks were often called governors.

In 1935, the Banking Act, which made significant changes to the structure and powers of the Federal Reserve, reorganized the Federal Reserve Board and changed the title of its members from "governors" to "members." However, the presidents of the regional Federal Reserve Banks continued to be referred to as "directors" until 1951, when their titles were changed to "presidents."

Today, the members of the Federal Reserve Board are referred to as "governors," while the presidents of the regional Federal Reserve Banks are referred to as "presidents." This terminology has been in use since the 1950s and reflects the current organizational structure of the Federal Reserve System.

Here are some interesting facts about the Federal Reserve that many people may not know:

1. The Federal Reserve was created in response to a series of financial panics and bank runs in the late 19th and early 20th centuries. The Fed was established to promote financial stability, provide liquidity to the banking system, and regulate the money supply.

2. The Federal Reserve System includes 12 regional Federal Reserve Banks, which are privately owned but subject to oversight by the Federal Reserve Board in Washington, D.C.

3. The Federal Reserve is the only central bank in the world that is divided into multiple regional banks, reflecting the decentralized structure of the US banking system.

4. The Federal Reserve's monetary policy decisions are made independently by the Federal Open Market Committee (FOMC), which includes both Federal Reserve Board members and regional Federal Reserve Bank presidents.

5. The Federal Reserve has a dual mandate to promote price stability and maximum employment. This means that the Fed aims to keep inflation low and stable while also promoting full employment.

6. The Federal Reserve has the power to create money, which it does by purchasing Treasury securities and other assets on the open market.

7. The Federal Reserve has a balance sheet of over $8 trillion, largely made up of Treasury securities and mortgage-backed securities.

8. The Federal Reserve is subject to regular audits and oversight by Congress, which helps ensure

      accountability and transparency.

9. The Federal Reserve also plays a key role in promoting financial stability by regulating and supervising banks and other financial institutions.

10. The Federal Reserve is one of the most important institutions in the global financial system and its decisions can have a significant impact on the US and global economies.

Ron Paul, a former US Congressman and presidential candidate, has been a vocal advocate for auditing the Federal Reserve. Paul has argued that the Fed's lack of transparency and accountability undermines the democratic process and allows the Fed to engage in policies that benefit special interests at the expense of the American people.

Paul's call for an audit of the Federal Reserve gained widespread support among some segments of the American public, including supporters of the Tea Party movement and other groups who were critical of government intervention in the economy.

In 2010, Congress passed the Dodd-Frank Wall Street Reform and Consumer Protection Act, which included a provision requiring the Government Accountability Office (GAO) to conduct an audit of the Federal Reserve's emergency lending facilities. This was the first time that an audit of the Fed had been mandated by Congress.

Since then, the GAO has conducted multiple audits of the Federal Reserve's operations, including its lending facilities and its oversight of financial institutions. However, some advocates for greater transparency and accountability continue to call for broader audits of the Fed, including its monetary policy decisions and its dealings with foreign central banks.

BANK OF JAPAN

The Bank of Japan (BoJ) is the central bank of Japan and one of the oldest central banks in the world. Here is some information about its history and role:

- The Bank of Japan was established in 1882 as a privately owned central bank with the goal of promoting economic development and stability. The Bank was nationalized in 1942 and became a government-owned entity.

- Like other central banks, the Bank of Japan has several key functions, including controlling the money supply, setting interest rates, and regulating financial institutions. The Bank also plays a key role in promoting financial stability and providing financial services to the government and financial institutions.

- The Bank of Japan is governed by a Board of Directors, which includes a Governor, two Deputy Governors, and six Executive Directors. The Governor is appointed by the Prime Minister of Japan and confirmed by the Diet (Japan's parliament).

- The Bank of Japan operates independently of political influence and is committed to achieving its mandate of maintaining price stability and promoting economic growth. In pursuit of these goals, the Bank has implemented a range of monetary policy measures, including quantitative easing and negative interest rates.

- The Bank of Japan is also responsible for maintaining financial stability in Japan through its regulation and supervision of financial institutions. The Bank conducts regular inspections of banks and other financial institutions to ensure their safety and soundness, and it has the power to intervene in financial markets to maintain stability if necessary.

- The Bank of Japan is one of the largest central banks in the world, with over 4,000 employees and a balance sheet of over 600 trillion yen. In addition to its monetary policy and financial stability functions, the Bank also provides financial services to the government and acts as a custodian of the country's foreign exchange reserves.

The BoJ has undergone significant changes over the years, both in terms of its institutional structure and its policies. Here are some key developments:

- Early years: The Bank of Japan was established in 1882 as a privately owned central bank with the goal of promoting economic development and stability. It was modeled in part on the Bank of England and other European central banks.

- World War II: During World War II, the Bank of Japan was nationalized and became a government-owned entity. In the postwar period, the Bank played a key role in Japan's reconstruction and economic growth.

- Bubble economy and bust: In the 1980s, Japan experienced a period of rapid economic growth, fueled in part by a speculative bubble in real estate and asset prices. However, this bubble eventually burst in the early 1990s, leading to a prolonged period of economic stagnation and deflation.

- Policy responses: In response to the economic challenges of the 1990s and 2000s, the Bank of Japan implemented a range of monetary policy measures, including zero interest rates, quantitative easing, and negative interest rates. The Bank also worked to promote financial stability and regulate financial institutions.

- Abenomics: In 2013, Japanese Prime Minister Shinzo Abe announced a set of economic policies known as "Abenomics," which included a range of fiscal and monetary measures aimed at promoting economic growth and ending deflation. The Bank of Japan played a key role in implementing these policies, including through its massive purchases of government bonds and other securities.

- Modernization: In recent years, the Bank of Japan has worked to modernize its operations and policies. This has included the introduction of a new monetary policy framework aimed at achieving a target inflation rate of 2%, as well as efforts to increase transparency and communication with the public.

The Bank of Japan has evolved over the years in response to changing economic conditions and policy priorities. While its institutional structure and policies have changed, the Bank's commitment to promoting economic stability and growth has remained a consistent theme throughout its history.

The BofJ is a government-owned entity, which means that it is not owned by private individuals or corporations. The Bank is overseen by a Board of Directors, which includes a Governor, two Deputy Governors, and six Executive Directors. The Governor is appointed by the Prime Minister of Japan and confirmed by the Diet (Japan's parliament).

As a central bank, the Bank of Japan does not exist to make a profit. Rather, its primary goals are to promote economic stability, maintain price stability, and ensure the smooth functioning of the financial system. To achieve these goals, the Bank uses a range of monetary policy tools, including setting interest rates, regulating financial institutions, and controlling the money supply.

While the Bank of Japan is not owned by private individuals or corporations, it does have some financial relationships with other entities. For example, the Bank holds government securities and other assets, and it provides financial services to the government and financial institutions. Additionally, the Bank's monetary policy decisions can have an impact on financial markets and the broader economy, which can affect the profits of businesses and individuals.

RESERVE BANK OF INDIA

The Reserve Bank of India (RBI) is the central bank of India and the primary regulator of the country's banking and financial system. Here are some key facts about the RBI:

- Establishment: The Reserve Bank of India was established on April 1, 1935, under the Reserve Bank of India Act, 1934. The Bank was established to regulate the currency and credit system, control the banking system, and promote economic growth and stability.

- Structure: The Reserve Bank of India is governed by a central board of directors, which includes a Governor, four Deputy Governors, and several other directors. The Governor is appointed by the Indian government, while the Deputy Governors are appointed by the RBI.

- Functions: The Reserve Bank of India has several key functions, including issuing and regulating the country's currency, maintaining price stability, supervising and regulating banks and financial institutions, and managing the country's foreign exchange reserves.

- Monetary policy: The Reserve Bank of India is responsible for setting monetary policy in India, including setting interest rates and controlling the money supply. The Bank uses a variety of tools to implement its monetary policy, including open market operations, reserve requirements, and liquidity adjustments.

- Financial stability: In addition to its monetary policy role, the Reserve Bank of India is also responsible for promoting financial stability in India. The Bank conducts regular inspections of banks and other financial institutions to ensure their safety and soundness, and it has the power to intervene in financial markets to maintain stability if necessary.

- International role: The Reserve Bank of India plays an important role in the international financial system. The Bank is a member of the International Monetary Fund, the Bank for International Settlements, and other international organizations, and it participates in various international initiatives to promote financial stability and cooperation.

The Reserve Bank of India is a key institution in the Indian economy and financial system, with broad responsibilities for promoting economic growth, maintaining price stability, and ensuring financial stability. The Bank's policies and decisions have a significant impact on India's economic development and on the lives of its citizens.

The RBI is a government-owned entity, which means that it is not owned by private individuals or corporations. The Bank is governed by a central board of directors, which includes a Governor, four Deputy Governors, and several other directors. The Governor is appointed by the Indian government, while the Deputy Governors are appointed by the RBI.

As a central bank, the Reserve Bank of India does not exist to make a profit. Rather, its primary goals are to promote economic growth and stability, maintain price stability, and ensure the smooth functioning of the financial system. To achieve these goals, the Bank uses a range of monetary policy tools, including setting interest rates, regulating financial institutions, and controlling the money supply.

While the Reserve Bank of India is not owned by private individuals or corporations, it does have some financial relationships with other entities. For example, the Bank holds government securities and other assets, and it provides financial services to the government and financial institutions. Additionally, the Bank's monetary policy decisions can have an impact on financial markets and the broader economy, which can affect the profits of businesses and individuals.

PEOPLE'S BANK
OF CHINA

The People's Bank of China (PBOC) is the central bank of the People's Republic of China and the primary regulator of China's banking and financial system. Here is a brief history of the Bank:

- Establishment: The People's Bank of China was established on December 1, 1948, shortly after the founding of the People's Republic of China. The Bank was established to promote economic development and stability and to serve as the central bank of the country.

- Early years: In the early years of the People's Bank of China, the Bank focused on promoting economic development and stability in the aftermath of World War II and the Chinese Civil War. The Bank played a key role in issuing currency, controlling the money supply, and regulating the banking system.

- Mao era: During the Mao era, the People's Bank of China played a central role in implementing the country's economic policies, including the Great Leap Forward and the Cultural Revolution. The Bank also played a key role in promoting economic self-reliance and reducing reliance on foreign capital and technology.

- Reform and opening up: In the 1980s and 1990s, China underwent a period of economic reform and opening up, during which the People's Bank of China played a key role in implementing monetary policy and promoting financial stability. The Bank also worked to modernize the country's financial system and to integrate China into the global economy.

- Recent developments: In recent years, the People's Bank of China has continued to play a key role in China's economic development and financial system. The Bank has implemented a range of monetary policy measures to promote economic growth and stability, including cutting interest rates and reserve requirements. The Bank has also worked to promote financial innovation and to regulate emerging financial technologies, such as blockchain and digital currencies.

The People's Bank of China has played a critical role in China's economic development and financial system since its establishment in 1948. The Bank's policies and decisions have had a significant impact on the country's economic growth, stability, and integration into the global economy.

The PBOC is a government-owned entity, which means that it is not owned by private individuals or corporations. The Bank is governed by the State Council of the People's Republic of China, which is the highest executive organ of the Chinese government. The Governor of the PBOC is appointed by the National People's Congress, which is China's highest legislative body.

As a central bank, the People's Bank of China does not exist to make a profit. Rather, its primary goals are to promote economic development and stability, maintain price stability, and ensure the smooth functioning of the financial system. To achieve these goals, the Bank uses a range of monetary policy tools, including setting interest rates, regulating financial institutions, and controlling the money supply.

While the People's Bank of China is not owned by private individuals or corporations, it does have some financial relationships with other entities. For example, the Bank holds government securities and other assets, and it provides financial services to the government and financial institutions. Additionally, the Bank's monetary policy decisions can have an impact on financial markets and the broader economy, which can affect the profits of businesses and individuals.

The PBOC owns US Treasuries, which are debt securities issued by the US government. According to the latest data from the US Department of the Treasury, China is currently the largest foreign holder of US Treasuries, with a total of over $1 trillion in holdings as of January 2022.

As a major global economy and a key trading partner of the United States, China has significant financial relationships with the US and other countries around the world. Owning US Treasuries allows China to invest its surplus funds in a relatively safe and liquid asset that provides a reliable source of income.

However, the PBOC's holdings of US Treasuries have also been a source of concern for some policymakers and analysts, who worry that China's significant holdings of US debt could give it undue influence over the US economy or make it vulnerable to changes in US economic policy.

The Chinese government issues and sells securities to fund its budget and other financial needs. The securities issued by the Chinese government include government bonds, treasury bills, and other debt securities, which are sold to domestic and foreign investors.

The Chinese government uses the proceeds from the sale of securities to fund various government programs, such as infrastructure development, social welfare, and military spending. These securities are also used to manage China's monetary policy and to regulate the country's financial system.

In recent years, China's securities market has undergone significant growth and development, with the government taking steps to liberalize the market and increase its integration with global financial markets. The Chinese government has also sought to expand the range of securities available to investors, including the introduction of new financial products such as municipal bonds, corporate bonds, and asset-backed securities.

The Chinese government issues and sells securities as an important tool for financing government activities and managing the country's financial system. The securities market in China is an important component of the country's broader economic and financial landscape, with significant implications for investors and the global economy.

The Federal Reserve (Fed) owns Chinese Government securities, along with other foreign government securities, as part of its broader holdings of foreign assets. These foreign securities are typically held as a means of managing the US dollar exchange rate and as a component of the Fed's broader monetary policy efforts.

The exact amount of Chinese Government securities held by the Fed is not publicly disclosed, as the Fed typically releases only aggregate data on its foreign asset holdings. However, it is known that China is a major holder of US Treasuries, which are the primary type of foreign government securities held by the Fed.

The US and China have a complex and interconnected financial relationship, with significant financial flows and holdings of assets between the two countries. While the Fed's holdings of Chinese Government securities may be relatively small in comparison to its other assets, they are nonetheless an important component of the broader financial ties between the US and China.

EUROPEAN CENTRAL BANK

The European Central Bank (ECB) is the central bank of the European Union and the primary monetary authority of the eurozone. Here is a brief history of the formation of the Bank:

- Treaty of Maastricht: The formation of the ECB was first proposed in the Treaty of Maastricht, which was signed in 1992 and established the European Union (EU) as a political and economic union. The Treaty laid the groundwork for a single currency, the euro, and called for the creation of a central bank to oversee monetary policy for the eurozone.

- The European Monetary Institute: In 1994, the European Monetary Institute (EMI) was established as a precursor to the ECB. The EMI was responsible for preparing for the introduction of the euro and overseeing the exchange rate mechanism.

- The ECB's establishment: The ECB was officially established on June 1, 1998, following the ratification of the Treaty of Amsterdam in 1997. The Bank is headquartered in Frankfurt, Germany, and is governed by a council of central bank governors from the 19 countries that use the euro as their currency.

- The euro's launch: On January 1, 1999, the euro was introduced as a virtual currency, with exchange rates fixed against other European currencies. The euro became a physical currency on January 1, 2002, when euro banknotes and coins were introduced.

- The ECB's role: The ECB is responsible for setting monetary policy for the eurozone, including setting interest rates and controlling the money supply. The Bank also oversees the eurozone's financial system and plays a key role in promoting economic growth and stability.

- Recent developments: In recent years, the ECB has faced a number of challenges, including managing the debt crisis in several eurozone countries and navigating the economic fallout from the COVID-19 pandemic. The Bank has implemented a range of monetary policy measures to support the eurozone economy, including cutting interest rates, providing liquidity to banks, and purchasing government bonds.

The European Central Bank plays a critical role in overseeing monetary policy and promoting economic growth and stability in the eurozone. The Bank's formation was a key milestone in the development of the European Union and the introduction of the euro as a single currency.

Critics of the European Central Bank (ECB) have raised a number of concerns about the Bank's policies and practices, particularly in the aftermath of the global financial crisis and the debt crisis in several eurozone countries. Some of the key criticisms of the ECB include:

1. Lack of accountability: Critics have argued that the ECB is insufficiently accountable to the public and to democratic institutions. The Bank is governed by a council of central bank governors, but critics argue that this structure gives too much power to unelected

officials and limits public oversight.

2. Over-reliance on monetary policy: Some analysts have criticized the ECB's over-reliance on monetary policy, particularly in the aftermath of the global financial crisis. Critics argue that the Bank has been too focused on keeping inflation low and has not done enough to promote economic growth and stability.

3. Austerity policies: The ECB has been criticized for its support of austerity policies in several eurozone countries, particularly Greece. Critics argue that these policies have exacerbated economic hardship and social inequality, and have failed to address underlying structural issues in these economies.

4. Lack of flexibility: Some analysts have criticized the ECB's lack of flexibility in responding to economic challenges, particularly the debt crisis in several eurozone countries. Critics argue that the Bank's rules and policies have limited its ability to respond to changing economic conditions and to support struggling economies.

5. Unequal distribution of benefits: The ECB's policies have been criticized for benefiting wealthier countries and individuals at the expense of poorer ones. Critics argue that the Bank's bond-buying program, for example, has primarily supported the bond markets of richer eurozone countries, while doing little to address underlying economic issues in struggling economies.

The ECB has faced significant criticism from some analysts and policymakers in recent years, particularly in the aftermath of the global financial crisis and the debt crisis in several eurozone countries. While the Bank has taken steps to address some of these concerns, it continues to be the subject of debate and controversy.

COMPARISON OF CENTRAL BANKS

Central banks play a critical role in the global economy, acting as the monetary authority in each country and overseeing the financial system. Among their key responsibilities are:

- Setting monetary policy: Central banks use a variety of tools to influence interest rates, money supply, and inflation in order to promote economic stability and growth.

- Maintaining financial stability: Central banks work to prevent and address financial crises, such as bank failures or asset bubbles, by monitoring and regulating financial institutions and markets.

- Issuing and managing currency: Central banks are responsible for issuing and managing the currency of their country, and may also hold foreign currency reserves.

- Serving as a lender of last resort: In times of financial stress, central banks may act as a lender of last resort to provide liquidity to the financial system and prevent a collapse of the banking system.

- Conducting international relations: Central banks may work with other central banks and international organizations to promote global economic stability and address common challenges.

There are several criticisms of central banking systems, including:

1. Lack of accountability: Central banks are often criticized for being too opaque and not sufficiently accountable to the public. Some argue that the central bank's independence can create a democratic deficit, limiting the ability of elected officials to influence monetary policy.

2. Political interference: While central banks are intended to be independent, there is always a risk that politicians may try to influence their decisions, potentially leading to politicized monetary policy that undermines economic stability.

3. Monetary policy effectiveness: Critics argue that central banks' monetary policy tools, such as interest rate adjustments and quantitative easing, may have limited effectiveness in influencing the economy, particularly in times of economic downturns.

4. Unequal distribution of benefits: Some argue that the benefits of central bank policies are often distributed unequally, with wealthier individuals and countries benefiting more than poorer ones.

5. Lack of flexibility: Central banks are often criticized for being too rigid and not adaptable enough to changing economic conditions. Some argue that central bank rules and policies may limit their ability to respond to changing economic environments.

6. Risk-taking behavior: Some analysts argue that central banks' efforts to stimulate economic growth and financial stability, such as through low interest rates and quantitative easing, may encourage risk-taking behavior and contribute to asset bubbles or financial

instability.

The Federal Reserve Bank of the United States was a privately owned institution, with ownership divided among member banks. The Bank of England was also privately owned until it was nationalized in 1946.

The Deutsche Bundesbank is also technically privately owned, as it is owned by the German regional banks known as the "Landesbanken." However, the Bundesbank is also closely tied to the German government and operates as part of the Eurosystem, which oversees monetary policy for the eurozone.

There are various differences in the governance structures of central banks around the world. Here are some key examples:

1. Independence: Some central banks are more independent than others in terms of their decision-making. For example, the Federal Reserve Bank of the United States is often cited as having a high degree of independence, while the People's Bank of China is more closely tied to the Chinese government.

2. Ownership: Central banks can be owned by the government, by private individuals or institutions, or a combination of the two. For example, the Bank of England was privately owned until it was nationalized in 1946, while the Federal Reserve Bank of the United States is privately owned by member banks.

3. Structure: The structure of central banks can vary widely. For example, the Federal Reserve Bank of the United States is a decentralized system of regional banks with a central governing board, while the Bank of Japan has a single central bank governor.

4. Transparency: The level of transparency of central

banks can also vary. Some central banks, such as the European Central Bank, are required to provide regular reports and disclosures, while others may be less transparent.

5. Accountability: Central banks can be accountable to a variety of stakeholders, including the government, the public, and financial institutions. For example, the Deutsche Bundesbank is accountable to the German government and the European Central Bank, while the Federal Reserve Bank of the United States is accountable to Congress.

6. Goals: Different central banks may have different goals and priorities in terms of their monetary policy. For example, the Federal Reserve Bank of the United States is focused on maintaining price stability and promoting economic growth, while the Reserve Bank of India has also prioritized financial inclusion and the development of the financial sector.

Independence

Central bank independence is the degree to which a central bank is free from political or other external influences in its decision-making. The level of independence can vary significantly between central banks and countries.

In the United States, the Federal Reserve Bank is often seen as a highly independent central bank. The Fed is a quasi-public institution that operates independently from the US government. While the President of the United States nominates the Chair of the Federal Reserve, once in office, the Chair and the Board of Governors are largely insulated from political pressure. This is seen as a way to promote stable and predictable monetary policy.

The Bank of England is also considered to be a highly independent central bank. After being nationalized in 1946, the Bank was given operational independence in 1997, meaning that it is free to set monetary policy without interference from the government. The Bank of England has a clear mandate to maintain price stability and has been given a high degree of autonomy to do so.

In contrast, the People's Bank of China is seen as being more closely tied to the Chinese government. The bank is part of the Chinese government and operates under its direction. The government appoints the bank's leadership and can influence its decision-making. However, in recent years, the bank has taken steps to increase its independence, such as by making monetary policy decisions based on economic data rather than political considerations.

The European Central Bank (ECB) is another central bank that is considered to be relatively independent. The bank is governed by a board of directors and has a mandate to maintain price stability in the eurozone. While the ECB is accountable to the European Parliament and other institutions, it operates independently from the national governments of the member states.

The Reserve Bank of India is also considered to be a relatively independent central bank. The bank is governed by a board of directors and has a mandate to maintain price stability while promoting economic growth. While the bank is accountable to the Indian government, it is largely free to make monetary policy decisions without political interference.

The Deutsche Bundesbank is also seen as an independent central bank, as it is owned by the German regional banks known as the "Landesbanken" rather than the German government. However, the bank is also closely tied to the German government and operates as part of the Eurosystem, which oversees monetary policy for the eurozone.

Ownership:

The ownership of central banks can also vary significantly between countries. Some central banks are owned by the government, while others are owned by private individuals or institutions. Here is a brief overview of the ownership structures of some of the central banks we have discussed.

The Federal Reserve Bank of the United States is a privately owned institution. It is owned by member banks, which are required to hold stock in the Federal Reserve. However, ownership of the Federal Reserve does not confer control over its decision-making. Instead, the Fed operates independently from its member banks and the government.

The Bank of England was also privately owned until it was nationalized in 1946. Today, the Bank is owned by the UK government, but it operates independently in its monetary policy decisions.

The Deutsche Bundesbank is technically privately owned, as it is owned by the German regional banks known as the "Landesbanken." However, the Bundesbank is closely tied to the German government and operates as part of the Eurosystem, which oversees monetary policy for the eurozone.

The People's Bank of China is owned by the Chinese government and operates under its direction. The bank is not publicly traded and there are no private shareholders.

The Reserve Bank of India is also owned by the Indian government. The bank is not publicly traded and there are no private shareholders.

The European Central Bank is also publicly owned, with the central banks of the eurozone member states holding shares in the bank. However, the ECB operates independently in its decision-making and is accountable to the European Parliament and other institutions.

Structures

The structure of central banks can vary widely between countries. Some central banks have a decentralized structure with multiple regional branches, while others have a more centralized structure with a single governing body. Here's an overview of the structure of some of the central banks we have discussed.

The Federal Reserve Bank of the United States has a decentralized structure. It is comprised of 12 regional banks, each with its own president and board of directors. The central governing board, known as the Federal Reserve Board, is based in Washington, D.C. and is responsible for making monetary policy decisions for the entire Federal Reserve System.

The Bank of England has a more centralized structure. It is governed by a Court of Directors, which is responsible for setting the Bank's strategy and policies. The Court of Directors is supported by a number of committees and advisory groups.

The Deutsche Bundesbank has a decentralized structure similar to the Federal Reserve Bank of the United States. It is comprised of nine regional branches, each with its own president and board of directors. The central governing board, known as the Executive Board, is responsible for making monetary policy decisions for the entire Bundesbank.

The People's Bank of China has a centralized structure. It is governed by a single central bank governor, who is responsible for making monetary policy decisions and overseeing the bank's operations.

The Reserve Bank of India has a decentralized structure. It is governed by a central board of directors, which is responsible for setting policy and making monetary policy decisions. The bank also has four regional offices and 19 regional branches.

The European Central Bank has a centralized structure. It is governed by a governing council, which is responsible for making monetary policy decisions for the entire eurozone. The governing council is made up of the central bank governors of the eurozone member states.

Transparency

Transparency is an important aspect of central bank governance. It allows for greater accountability and helps to promote confidence in the bank's decision-making processes. Here is an overview of the transparency of some of the central banks we have discussed.

The Federal Reserve Bank of the United States is required by law to report to Congress on its monetary policy decisions twice a year. The bank also releases minutes of its Federal Open Market Committee meetings and publishes an annual report outlining its activities and financial performance.

The Bank of England is required to publish quarterly inflation reports, which provide an overview of the bank's economic outlook and its monetary policy decisions. The bank also publishes the minutes of its Monetary Policy Committee meetings and an annual report.

The Deutsche Bundesbank is required to provide regular reports on its activities and financial performance. The bank also publishes an annual report and provides regular statements on its monetary policy decisions.

The People's Bank of China has become more transparent in recent years. The bank now publishes regular reports on its monetary policy decisions and financial performance. However, it is still considered to be less transparent than some other central banks.

The Reserve Bank of India publishes quarterly reports on its monetary policy decisions and economic outlook. The bank also provides regular updates on its activities and financial performance.

The European Central Bank is required to publish regular reports on its monetary policy decisions and provide regular updates on its activities and financial performance. The bank also publishes minutes of its governing council meetings and an annual report.

Accountability

Accountability is an important aspect of central bank governance. It helps to ensure that central banks are operating in the public interest and are being held responsible for their actions. Here's an overview of the accountability of some of the central banks we have discussed.

The Federal Reserve Bank of the United States is accountable to the US Congress. The Chair of the Federal Reserve is required to testify before Congress twice a year on the bank's monetary policy decisions and its activities. The bank is also subject to audits by the Government Accountability Office.

The Bank of England is accountable to the UK government. The bank is required to report regularly to the government on its activities and its monetary policy decisions. The bank is also subject to audits by the National Audit Office.

The Deutsche Bundesbank is accountable to the German government. The bank is required to provide regular reports on its activities and financial performance to the government. The bank is also subject to audits by the German Federal Court of Audit.

The People's Bank of China is accountable to the Chinese government. The bank is required to report regularly to the government on its activities and its monetary policy decisions. However, the government has been criticized for its lack of transparency in its oversight of the bank.

The Reserve Bank of India is accountable to the Indian government. The bank is required to report regularly to the government on its activities and its monetary policy decisions. The bank is also subject to audits by the Comptroller and Auditor General of India.

The European Central Bank is accountable to the European Parliament and other institutions. The bank is required to report regularly to the Parliament on its activities and its monetary policy decisions. The bank is also subject to audits by the European Court of Auditors.

Goals

The goals of central banks can vary depending on the country and the economic conditions that they are facing. However, central banks generally share a mandate to promote price stability and economic growth. Here is an overview of the goals of some of the central banks we have discussed.

The Federal Reserve Bank of the United States has a dual mandate to promote price stability and maximum employment. The bank aims to keep inflation low and stable, while also promoting full employment and economic growth.

The Bank of England also has a dual mandate to promote price stability and support economic growth. The bank aims to keep inflation at a target rate of 2% and supports economic growth by providing liquidity to the financial system.

The Deutsche Bundesbank aims to promote price stability and maintain the stability of the financial system. The bank aims to keep inflation at a target rate of below 2%, while also promoting the stability of the banking system and the broader financial sector.

The People's Bank of China aims to promote price stability and support economic growth. The bank aims to keep inflation at a target rate of around 3%, while also supporting the growth of the Chinese economy.

The Reserve Bank of India aims to promote price stability and support economic growth. The bank aims to keep inflation at a target rate of 4% and supports economic growth by providing liquidity to the financial system.

The European Central Bank also has a mandate to promote price stability. The bank aims to keep inflation at a target rate of below 2%. The bank also supports economic growth by providing liquidity to the financial system and supporting the stability of the eurozone.

The similarities and differences in the goals, structures, transparency, and accountability of central banks can have important implications for the global economy and for policymakers. The similarities in goals, such as promoting price stability and economic growth, can help to promote consistency in monetary policy across countries. This can help to promote stability in the global economy and prevent imbalances that could cause financial crises.

At the same time, the differences in the structures, transparency, and accountability of central banks can make it more difficult to coordinate monetary policy across countries. Different central banks may have different views on the appropriate level of interest rates or the best way to support economic growth. This can create challenges for policymakers, who need to balance the needs of their own economy with the needs of the global economy.

The ownership structures of central banks can also have important implications for the global economy. Privately-owned central banks, for example, may have different incentives and priorities than publicly-owned central banks. This can create challenges for policymakers, who need to ensure that the central bank is acting in the public interest.

Measures

The largest central banks in the world can be measured in different ways, depending on the criteria used. Here are some possible ways to measure the size of central banks:

1. Total assets: One way to measure the size of a central bank is by its total assets. This includes all the assets held by the central bank, including government securities, foreign exchange reserves, and loans to financial institutions. According to data from the International Monetary Fund (IMF) as of 2021, the five largest central banks by total assets are:

- People's Bank of China: $6.6 trillion
- Federal Reserve System (US): $8.2 trillion
- European Central Bank: $8.6 trillion
- Bank of Japan: $5.5 trillion
- Bank of England: $0.6 trillion

2. Foreign exchange reserves: Another way to measure the size of a central bank is by its foreign exchange reserves, which are holdings of foreign currencies that can be used to stabilize exchange rates and support international trade. According to IMF data as of 2021, the five largest holders of foreign exchange reserves are:

- People's Bank of China: $3.2 trillion
- Bank of Japan: $1.4 trillion
- European Central Bank: $0.9 trillion
- Federal Reserve System (US): $0.3 trillion
- Bank of Russia: $0.6 trillion

3. Gold reserves: A third way to measure the size of a central bank is by its gold reserves, which are holdings of gold that can be used as a store of value and to support the currency. According to World Gold Council data as of 2021, the five largest holders of gold reserves are:

- United States: 8,134 tonnes
- Germany: 3,362 tonnes
- International Monetary Fund: 2,814 tonnes
- Italy: 2,451 tonnes
- France: 2,436 tonnes

These rankings can change over time as central banks adjust their holdings and as exchange rates fluctuate.

CONCLUSION

Here are a few interesting facts about central banks that you may not have heard before:

- The Swiss National Bank is one of the few central banks in the world that is publicly traded. This means that anyone can buy shares in the bank and potentially profit from its activities.

- The Bank of Japan has been buying Japanese government bonds as part of its quantitative easing program for years. In fact, the bank now holds more than 40% of all Japanese government bonds outstanding.

- The European Central Bank is the only central bank in the world that is responsible for monetary policy for an entire currency area, rather than just one country. This makes its decision-making process more complex than that of many other central banks.

- The Reserve Bank of New Zealand was the first central bank in the world to adopt an inflation targeting framework. This approach has since been adopted by many other central banks around the world.

- The Federal Reserve Bank of the United States has a unique structure that includes 12 regional banks, each with its own president and board of directors. This structure helps to ensure that the bank is responsive to regional economic conditions.

- The People's Bank of China is the largest central bank

in the world in terms of assets. It holds more than \$5 trillion in foreign currency reserves and plays a key role in managing the Chinese economy.

- The Bank of Canada is one of the few central banks in the world that has not changed its inflation target since it was first introduced in the 1990s. The bank's target is to keep inflation at 2%, and it has been successful in meeting this target for many years.

Central banks are a vital component of the global economy, influencing economic growth, employment, and price stability. From the Federal Reserve Bank in the United States to the Bank of Japan and the European Central Bank, each central bank has its own unique history, governance structure, and approach to achieving its goals. Through this book, we have explored the origins and evolution of several key central banks, including their goals, structures, transparency, accountability, and ownership.

While central banks have played an essential role in maintaining global economic stability, they have also faced criticisms and challenges. These include issues related to their independence, transparency, and accountability, as well as the impact of globalization on their operations. Nevertheless, central banks continue to adapt and innovate, exploring new tools and strategies to address these challenges and promote economic growth and stability.

Bank of the United States

The Bank of the United States was a national bank that was chartered by the U.S. Congress in 1791 at the request of Alexander Hamilton, the first Secretary of the Treasury. The bank was created to serve as a central repository for federal funds and to provide stability to the emerging American financial system.

The Bank of the United States was headquartered in Philadelphia and had branches in several major cities, including New York, Boston, and Baltimore. It was given the power to issue bank notes, make loans, and accept deposits, and it quickly became a major player in the American economy.

The bank's charter was controversial from the start, with many Americans opposing the idea of a national bank. Some felt that the bank was unconstitutional, while others feared that it would give too much power to the federal government. Despite the opposition, the bank's charter was renewed in 1816 for another 20 years.

In 1832, President Andrew Jackson vetoed a bill to renew the bank's charter, arguing that the bank was too powerful and too closely aligned with the interests of wealthy elites. Jackson's veto was upheld by Congress, and the bank was eventually dissolved in 1836.

The Bank of the United States played an important role in the development of American finance and helped establish the country's creditworthiness on an international level. However, its controversial history and eventual dissolution illustrate the ongoing tension between centralized power and states' rights in American politics.

The Bank of the United States is often referred to as the first central bank of the United States, but the term "central bank" is somewhat imprecise and can be interpreted in different ways.

If we define a central bank as an institution that serves as a lender of last resort, issues currency, manages the money supply, and acts as a regulatory authority for the banking system, then the Bank of the United States can be considered a precursor to modern central banks.

The Bank of the United States had the power to issue bank notes, regulate the money supply, and provide loans to other banks in times of crisis. However, its regulatory authority over the banking system was limited, and it did not have a monopoly on issuing currency.

In this sense, the Bank of the United States was more of a hybrid institution, combining elements of a central bank and a commercial bank. It played an important role in stabilizing the American financial system during its early years, but it was not a fully developed central bank in the way that we understand the term today.

ACKNOWLEDGEMENT

Cover Image: PUBLIC DOMAIN Front entrance of the Marriner S. Eccles building built in 1937. File:Ec 8 (26088200676).jpg Created: 29 March 2011

Image 1: PUBLIC DOMAIN Sealing of the Bank of England Charter 1694 by Lady Jane-Lindsay 1905 Created January 1 1905

Image 2: PUBLIC DOMAIN Bank of Japan headquarters in Tokyo, Japan Created 28 January 2007

Sources for more information on central banks:

1. "The Alchemists: Three Central Bankers and a World on Fire" by Neil Irwin (2013) - This book explores the lives and careers of three central bankers - Ben Bernanke, Jean-Claude Trichet, and Mervyn King - who played key roles in responding to the global financial crisis of 2008. The author examines the decisions they made and the impact they had on the global economy.

2. "Central Banking in Theory and Practice" by Alan S. Blinder (2019) - This book provides an overview of the theory and practice of central banking, covering topics such as monetary policy, financial stability, and the relationship between central banks and governments. The author draws on his own experience as a former vice chairman of the Federal Reserve to provide practical insights into the challenges facing central banks today.

3. "The Power and Independence of the Federal Reserve" by Peter Conti-Brown (2016) - This book examines the history and governance of the Federal Reserve Bank, focusing on the relationship between the central bank and the US government. The author argues that the Federal Reserve has become too powerful and too independent, and calls for greater oversight and accountability.

4. "Central Banks at a Crossroads: What Can We Learn from History?" by Michael D. Bordo and Ã˜yvind Eitrheim (2016) - This book provides a historical overview of central banking, focusing on the evolution of central banks over the past century. The authors explore the challenges facing central banks today and draw on lessons from history to suggest potential solutions.

5. "The House of Rothschild: Money's Prophets, 1798-1848" by Niall Ferguson - This book provides an in-depth look at the history of the Rothschild family and their rise to prominence as one of the most powerful financial dynasties in Europe.

6. "The World's Banker: A Story of Failed States, Financial Crises, and the Wealth and Poverty of Nations" by Sebastian Mallaby - This book provides a broader perspective on the role of global finance and the history of central banking, with a focus on the Rothschilds' involvement in the development of the global financial system.